Snatched Out
Thrown In

Venasta D. Parsons

TaylorMade Publishing
www.taylormadepublishing.com

Snatched Out Thrown In
Venasta D. Parsons
Copyright © December 2022
All rights reserved
ISBN: 978-1-953526-50-2

Table of Contents

Forward...i

Dedication..ii

Chapter 1 My Mother's Life (Who was she?)...................... 1

Chapter 2 Plucked From the Familiar.................................. 3

Chapter 3 Foster Care Nightmare 8

Chapter 4 Our Second Foster Home, Permanent?............. 14

Chapter 5 Teen and High School Life 18

Chapter 6 My First Real Detour 22

Chapter 7 Army Life.. 25

Chapter 8 Being Me and Living Free 28

Chapter 9 Being a Military Wife 32

Chapter 10 More Painful Infidelity.................................... 37

Chapter 11 Georgia Life 40

Chapter 12 Final Betrayal.. 42

Chapter 13 Temptation Alley 46

Chapter 14 Temporary Fairytale.. 50

Chapter 15 Rough Terrain 52

Chapter 16 Health Scare 55

Special Thanks.. 58

GOD'S AMAZING PLAN UNFOLDS!! 59

About the Author 60

Forward

This book consists of different phases of my foster life events such as; hurt, pain, embarrassment and shame which made me; MAD, ANGRY, and BITTER! Being snatched out of situations brought healing and living in the end!! When I started to write this I was 54 years young of course and now finishing it all up, I am presently 59 years young!

The beginning age of my memories was six; my life took a traumatic journey which filled my head with questions concerning family love which also dominated my life for years. Though quite painful and disgusting at times it has led me straight to the destination GOD had for me all along; Healed, Whole, and Free. I was healed from all of the "snatched out" encounters and made whole from all of the "thrown in" situations; finally free to live life with the ability to give and receive real Love again.

The names I will be using are real so I will refer to an initial and sometimes their last names. It is not hard to remember and share the truth when it is the truth. While writing this, I experienced many tears because I could actually see in my mind the things that took place beginning at the age of six. Some of the memories were so vivid that I had to say, "Wow, this really happened!" I am not afraid to share major events of my life's story. I am totally free from all of the shame, embarrassment, bitterness and anger. I pray that this book will help all who read it in some area of their family life, and make them stronger and more confident in receiving and giving LOVE.

Dedication

I dedicate this book is to my dear brother, Terry, who traveled the "road of foster care" with me. I am so proud that he is my brother and living life beyond the hurt, pain, embarrassment, and shame! He endured the foster care system with many tears, rejection and pain but now he is an awesome conqueror and lives life to the fullest. You were my baby brother then and I will continue to love you and hold your hand whenever you need me! I LOVE YOU!

Linda and Ann, thank you for helping me to become the woman I am today, a woman with integrity and wisdom! You helped raise me and continue to be in my life to this day. Linda and Ann, you will never know the powerful impact you made in my life, I love you always!

I wish to thank my fantastic four seeds for they are my greatest joy in life; Tenesa, Terry Jr. Shanae and Emmanuel, my four and no more!! The joy of carrying you and seeing you grow from infants, toddlers, teens to adults was quite a miracle. Three of you were C-sections, only one was natural and I must say that's why she is the older bossy one and it will never change! I love you all to life!

A huge THANK YOU for my great editors, retired educator, Deb Waller and the most dynamic author/writer I've ever met, Frizella Taylor, the Lord blessed me tremendously with these two women who assisted me many times both patiently and lovingly!

Chapter 1 My Mother's Life (Who was she?)

I want to take this time to explain what I knew about my mother. I do not want to make her sound like a hideous monster, even though we thought she was! My mother's life was jacked up. I found all of this out after I was grown. She was the oldest of four; there was one boy and three girls. She lived with her parents and her mother was an alcoholic. She would drink something called "Explode" and one day she, my grandmother, came in after drinking and laid on the couch. Everyone thought she was sleeping and they went to bed but never checked on her.

That morning, she did not wake up, they discovered she had died in her sleep on the couch and I guess that had to be an ugly shock for her and her siblings. I am not sure how old my mother was when that happened. Since she was the oldest that meant she had to help with taking care of her brother and sisters. I cannot imagine the fear, hurt and pain she must have gone through. I guess that is one reason why she did not know how to love or show real love.

My mother never shared a lot about her family with me. I do not know if my grandfather ever married someone else or not. However, we all lived together, he and a lady I called grandmother and they were nice to us. I did not know that my mother's siblings, our aunts and uncle, were not active in our lives until we were up in age. Aunt Jamesena was the only one who would come visit us when we were in the projects, she spoiled us. Terry and I wished she was our mother.

I am not sure if my mother ever finished high school, but, I would never ask those questions. Now that we are adults, I know that she had worked as a cook in the public school system and was an outstanding cook. She retired from that and became a school crossing guard. Now this was way funny to me; how about she was 75 and worked at a school as a "FOSTER GRANDMOTHER" can you believe that? She helped the teachers with their classes for kindergarten and preschool, and all I can say about that was WHAT? REALLY? So, you never know how people are going to turn things around in their life.

My mother had two more children; their father was Mr. P. So my step sister and brother never grew up with Terry and I. My mother was married once to a man named Mr. Jim G. and he was in a wheelchair with no legs. We were older during that time and they lived in the projects on College Street.

My mother did not keep in contact with us as we continued our lives in foster care; however, she kept and raised our other two siblings. We never had any kind of celebrations with them, but as we all got older, we were able to talk to each other over the phone.

My sister, Cassandra, has lived with our mother since she was born and she still does to this day. My brother Khristian also lived with them, but he got involved in street activities and spent many years in jail and ended up with a life sentence in prison. He was murdered in prison during the month of April, 2011. So this is what I know about my mother and her other children, our siblings that she decided to keep. Maybe giving us away was the best thing that could have happened to us. My brother Terry spent a lot of his young life in the prison system. After serving his time, he is now a productive, working, well-functioning man living in Tennessee.

Chapter 2 Plucked From the Familiar

I was born in Knoxville, Tennessee on January 5th, 1960. It's a shame that I have no baby pictures to share, I don't know why, however, I can remember my life stages starting when I was six living in the projects of Mechanicsville. I can still see those stone steps my brother and I used to play on; running up and down until one day when I fell and busted my forehead open, talk about painful. I remember my mother being upset because they had to call an ambulance to take me to the hospital and the doctors stitched up my forehead. After that I was treated special but I couldn't go out to play or walk up and down the steps for a while.

I can remember my grandparents being there with us. We would walk across the railroad track to go to the market and buy brown eggs and bottled milk. My brother and I were close and played together outside often. I had some friends at our elementary school, Maynard Elementary, who were always playing with us and sat with us in the lunchroom. They never made fun of us for being on "free lunch" which meant we had a special coin that was used to pay instead of real money.

There were many other kids using free lunch so I didn't feel like I was any less than anyone else. One day we moved to another section of town to Moriah St. We were glad that they didn't have steps to climb up. We lived in a court area which meant that there was only one way in and one way out. Our mother had finally moved us into her own apartment. She was pretty nice most of the time but complained a lot of being "tired of these kids". She wasn't very loving and I don't remember receiving hugs from her. I can imagine now that living in the projects with two children was sometimes depressing for her. She wasn't married to our father but she had a boyfriend named Mr. P.

Our father was good to us, he visited us a lot and took us out to eat and bought us ice cream at Kay's Ice cream. Everyone in the neighborhood knew that we were Jessie Williams' children. He carried his 32 revolver in the glove compartment of his car. He told us if anyone ever bothered us or tried to hurt us we better tell him and they would have to deal with him. It was always such a happy time when we were with our father. He had a good job as a steel supply cutter and he took us to meet his boss and other men who worked there. Being with our father was the greatest feeling in the world! Our mother's boyfriend, Mr. P., wasn't too friendly towards us but he treated us okay.

Once he did something pretty mean to my brother. We only had one bathroom and I was in it, my brother had to pee and he couldn't wait for me to finish; so he peed in a shoe box. That was a bad day for us because my mother was angry. I remember how she and Mr. P. yelled a lot at me and my brother. Then, mom picked up a clear glass ashtray and hit my brother in the head; Mr. P. slapped him on the butt and threatened to whip him with his belt. I think that's the day I began to realize how much I hated both of them. I rose up and screamed, "I'm going to tell my daddy!"

Every time my mother would fuss at us about anything I always would say to her, "I am going to tell my daddy"; she would end up sending me upstairs to my room. The emotional and verbal abuse was real in my life. She would tell us daily how she was "sick and tired of us", "we would never amount to anything", "y'all make me sick" and how she "wished we were with our father. Wow, she didn't know how bad we wished that too! Sometimes she would be nice to us but it didn't last long. If we spilled water in the kitchen or dropped something, the demeaning words would flow. "Stupid" was the name we heard most.

When we saw our daddy again, I told him what happened to Terry and he came over and threatened Mr. P. with his gun. My daddy told him, "If he ever put his hands on us he would kill him", and we were so happy to know that. It may sound mean but honestly, we didn't like our mother or Mr. P. After I turned seven years of age, I had a nice birthday celebration with my daddy and brother, my mother had a lady to come over and pierce my ears. Her name was Ms. M. Warren.

It was a scary experience! She put a needle on the stove eye and applied ice cubes to my ears so they became numb enough that when she stuck the needle in my ear with the thread, it did not hurt. She tied it at the end and applied Vaseline. I was happy my ears were pierced because I knew that my auntie was going to buy me some small, real gold, earrings from Miller's Department Store. She promised to get them once I had my ears pierced.

We had the best auntie in the state of Tennessee! She would buy us Levi jeans and Converse All Star high top sneakers. She didn't have any children so she spoiled us real good. Sometimes when we spent the night with her, we prayed and wished we could live with her!! Little did we know the big shock that was coming up a few weeks after my birthday! It all started with Mr. P and our mother sitting in the kitchen talking real loud one day. For our dinner, she prepared spaghetti and crackers instead of our usual Beanie Weenie and saltine crackers.

It's funny how I can actually see myself eating that and enjoying it! Every Sunday my mother always had big dinners. She was a great cook and that was our last dinner with her. One thing for sure is that we were never hungry and she let us eat snacks whenever we wanted. Continuing on with what took place on that particular day, our mother told us that we were going to be moving and we had to pack up our clothes and shoes in a large trash bag and be ready the next day for the move.

So we were a little scared because we didn't know where we were going or who was taking us. At first, my brother and I were thinking that our daddy was coming to get us to live with him. That night all we talked about was the good times we were going to have and all the fun things we would do living with our daddy. I was so glad that I would be leaving that place. The morning came and we got dressed up in Sunday clothes and I had my new earrings that my auntie had given me for my seventh birthday in my ears.

After eating our last breakfast with our mom, she told us that we needed to call our daddy at work because we would never see him again. I was so sad to hear that. She gave me the phone to call him, when his boss answered, I told him who I was and that I needed to talk to my daddy because we were moving. So he got our daddy on the phone. That was the scariest phone call, my brother and I cried because daddy told us he couldn't get to us until later that evening. Mom had told us to go sit outside on the sidewalk, she walked us out and left us sitting there alone.

Terry was crying, as we sat there I hugged him and I just held his hand and told him that we would be okay because daddy would come and find us wherever we were. A car pulled up and a white lady got out, she came right to us and smiled. She told us her name and that she was taking us to a nice home. She had a shiny badge on and a black briefcase with papers sticking out. I remember because some papers fell out and I jumped up to get them for her. She hugged me and then went into the apartment. Terry and I sat outside for a little while longer and talked about where we might be going. We both wanted it to be a nice house with a swing set and a nice yard.

I just kept telling him we will always be together and daddy will find us! When our mother called for us to come inside, the lady had started picking up our bags of clothes. I had two bags of clothes and one bag with my shoes and so did my brother. The lady told us her name, Ms. Pam Peace, and that she was our social worker. Of course we didn't know what that meant, but we were so glad to be leaving that place it really didn't matter.

Our mother didn't hug us nor kiss us goodbye, she just said bye and told the lady to "take them on" waved her hand and went back in the apartment. Once we finished putting our things in the car Ms. P. put us in the back seat and told us not to be worried because she was taking us to a really nice home and family across town. Neither one of us cried anymore, we were too excited about our new family and home. The ride was quite comfortable, we played tic-tac-toe.

Chapter 3 Foster Care Nightmare

Little did we know, the place she was taking us to turned out to be a big building! I thought of it as a prison or something like that, but it was the Children Social Services building. She took us in there and we met lots of people. They had a lot of offices and an elevator. Ms. P. told us that we would only be there 24 hours and then go to our new home. The room they took us to had beds and other children there. We stayed close to each other. She took us to meet some of the workers there, they all had on badges too.

People were very nice and some gave us hugs. Some of the children were playing with toys and others were sitting on the big rug watching TV on the floor. No one seemed to be sad or crying. I thought this was a safe place where all of us go before we are taken to our new homes and families. They explained to us that we were considered "foster children". I wasn't really sure what that meant, but all of the kids there had the same title.

Ms. P. had placed our clothes bags beside two twin beds and took us all around the place. The hallways were long and it reminded me of a hospital because it smelled like Lysol, oh yes I do remember that. We ate and slept in our room. The room was set up where my brother's bed was right beside mine and I think we were quite satisfied with that. Here we were once again; snatched out of familiar surroundings and thrown into a system we knew absolutely nothing about.

The next day was very busy for us, the staff came by and woke us up at different times. We got dressed, ate breakfast and then we were taken into a big room. Some of the children were hugging and talking to their family members. They had a large sign on the door that said something like, Private Family. We didn't know who was coming to see us, but I thought it would be our auntie; no, it was our daddy! We screamed and ran to him. That was one of the best times ever!

He said that he wanted us to live with him but some court people said he had to have a wife and he wasn't married. While we were sitting on his lap this little girl came up and wanted my daddy to pick her up. I had a fit and told her that he wasn't her daddy, but mine! My daddy told me not to be so mean because she probably doesn't have a daddy, so we had to be friendly towards her. I felt so bad later because I was being selfish. My brother and I had a great daddy and we didn't even realize how important that was until years later.

When daddy left, Ms. P. came and told us we were going to our new family home. She drove us to a nice neighborhood, the street was named McCalla Ave. The house was nice with a small porch. The man who opened the door was very tall and dark. He invited us all in and called for a lady named Ms. C. She was his wife and they seemed to be happy that we were there and they were waiting for us. We all sat in the living room. He told us his name was Mr. F. and his wife is Ms. C. He sat in a big lazy boy chair and we were on the couch, it was a nice room. As we sat we held hands, something my brother and I did a lot. Ms. P. talked to them about us and they just smiled and said yes.

Ms. P. brought our clothes in and they took the bags in a bedroom where they said we would be sleeping. There were two beds and a big closet but only one big dresser with a mirror. Ms. P. hugged us and told us that our father knew where we were and would be calling us on the phone but we had to go to that other place to visit with him. She left us there and we both cried a little because she had been so nice to us and I was afraid we might not ever see her again now that we were with this new family.

Life started out good when we first got situated. Mr. F. worked every day and Ms. C. stayed home and watched TV a lot. She smoked cigarettes and so did he. She kept a big can of Lysol in the living room but sometimes we could still smell the cigarette smoke. Things were fun most of the time and we were the only kids in the house. Later, we met some other kids in the neighborhood. We played outside in the backyard where we had a huge cherry tree and there was a fence around the yard, so we felt pretty safe. There was an alley and sometimes a lot of cats would jump the fence and come in our yard.

Once, I climbed the tree and fell and sprained my ankle; we later discovered a small stick got stuck in it. I had crutches for a little while. Ms. C. took me to the hospital and was quite caring towards me. Our birthdays were always celebrated with cake and gifts, they showed us a lot of love.

They enrolled us in school where we met some good friends. The teachers treated us nice and didn't address us as "foster children". Then, one day things changed for us; our foster parents had a little girl who started living with us and her name was Debbie.

She was a foster kid too, younger than us, about four and she sucked on her fingers. She was really pretty, fair-skinned, with good hair, she looked mixed. Ms. C. started treating us like crap. She began calling us black and ignorant and told us that nobody would ever want us because our own mother didn't even want us. I couldn't figure out what had caused her to change towards us. By my 10th birthday things began to go downhill for us.

My brother and I developed a plan to get snacks at night without getting caught. I would go to the refrigerator and he would go to the bathroom. We would count to three and my brother would flush the toilet while I would open the fridge and take out a piece of bologna and a piece of cheese. Then we would run back to our room and divide it and eat it. Wow, we did this a lot and never got caught. Debbie was always getting her way, but Mr. F. and Ms. C. didn't cater to us like they used to.

One day my brother and I didn't want to eat something Ms. C. had cooked and she became angry with us. She made us go to our rooms and told Mr. Frank that we were ungrateful little bad asses. That was the only time I can remember her saying that to us. The emotional abuse started daily. She would curse us by reminding us that we were "no good" and that no one would ever want us and that we were trash. I was so mad and I told my brother I was going to tell our daddy on our next visit.

We didn't like them as much anymore and we used to wish she would die in her sleep and that Mr. F. would get a nice wife. Yes, it sounds mean, but it's the way we felt about her. One day my brother had eaten something from a bowl then hid it under his bed instead of washing it. When she found it, she told Mr. F. to whip him with a belt and he held my brother upside down and whipped him on his naked behind with a belt. He gave him about 5 licks, it didn't last long, but we both cried. I yelled out to them that I was going to tell my daddy! They must have gotten scared because after that incident they never touched us again.

We spent more time in our room and didn't talk to them much at all. I read a lot of nursery rhymes to my brother. We played with Legos a lot, building homes that we wanted to live in when we grew up. I just hated them both! I couldn't wait for our next visit with our dad at that building. I told him what happened to Terry and how they were talking to us. He was very upset and told us that he will see to it that we are put in another foster home. We also told Ms. P. and she promised to find us another foster home.

I had bad memories of my tenth birthday. We had cake and balloons, but Mr. F. and Ms. C. didn't get me any gifts and that was ok because that was my last birthday spent in that house. Moving out day finally arrived for me and my brother! That night we had packed up our clothes and we had suitcases this time and many more clothes and shoes. We were so happy to be leaving that house, I think we went to bed singing that song, "Oh Happy Day."

Ms. P. came to get us, Mr. F. and Ms. C. had us dress in our nice church clothes earlier that morning. I should have known they were up to something. The Sunday before we left their house they took us to church and asked the pastor and some others to pray for us because we were going to be leaving their home. They acted like they were a little sad but we knew they were faking it. We never disrespected them but I would always tell them that "I am telling my daddy" whenever Ms. C. would talk ugly to us. My brother never said anything he would just drop his head. Once we started saying that Ms. C. was an ugly witch! So, every time she said mean words to us we would just laugh and she would call us crazy kids.

Our big day of freedom came, Ms. Pam came to get us and we didn't hug them or say goodbye, we just left. But they let Debbie hug us and she cried a little. I felt sorry for her because we didn't know how they would treat her after we left. Being ten gave me a new awareness of life that gave me control of how people treated me. I can't explain it, but I was never afraid of them, I just couldn't stand them when they started treating us mean.

We were riding across town and we pulled onto a street called Castle St. I really thought we would see castles and that our new home would have a king and a queen as our foster parents and we would be the prince and princess. We pulled up to a really big green house with a long porch and nice front yard. We felt so excited! We kept saying "look at that" and pointing at different things. Ms. Pam laughed with us and was also singing the song, "Oh Happy Day"- we just made up our own version.

Chapter 4 Our Second Foster Home, Permanent?

Wow what a huge house! The door had a black gate over it and they had a doorbell, this caused us to really think this was a castle. We just stood there on the front porch holding hands as usual while Ms. P. rang the doorbell. A lady answered who had on an apron and her hair was up in a bun. She welcomed us in and led us to the living room which was really big too. People were sitting there and they all welcomed us and came to hug us, some even kissed us on the forehead, it was totally amazing!

One lady told us she was our Aunt Gertrude, another lady said she was our Aunt Sylvine, and the oldest lady said she was Mother Dear, our new mother. The other two ladies were Ms. Bea and Ms. Iona. There was a man, named Mr. Charlie, who said he is our Uncle Charlie. They were just like a real family and they included us as if we were their children. Terry and I hugged them all and believe it or not, it did feel like we were in a loving home. They talked to Ms. P. for a while and the lady named Ms. Bea took us in the kitchen where they had food for us. The kitchen was big and well stocked with food, she told us we could eat as much as we wanted. Ms. P. hugged us and told us she would be checking on us once a month, but if we needed her we could call her.

The start of a beautiful family relationship was coming to life. We went back into the living room and they all kept telling us how glad they were that we were there. The family name was Freeman and it consisted of the older mother, two grown daughters, their nephew and two other women that lived there.

Aunt Gertrude worked for the city welfare office, Aunt Sylvine was a nurse, and Uncle Charlie was a cook/waiter at a restaurant called Steak & Ale. Ms. Iona and Ms. Bea were tenants there. I was too surprised for words, I felt like screaming a big "thank you" to all of them, but I just sat and held my brother's hand. One of the aunties showed us the house, they had an upstairs where my bed was; in the same room with Aunt Gertrude. There were two other bedrooms and a bathroom.

The living room had a guest room beside it and there was a big dining room with "Mother Dear's" bedroom right across from it. There were two bathrooms on this floor and downstairs was a big basement. Something called a furnace was there along with a bathroom and a beauty shop! Another three bedrooms were there also; this house was humongous to us. Terry slept downstairs and he liked it. This house was beautiful, they had a large picture window with long hanging curtains, and it felt so good being there.

Well life was going quite wonderful. This family was a blessing for real. Some of the things they did was to enroll us in the Y.M.C.A. where we took swimming lessons and dance. They even had a piano and I started taking piano lessons! For school enrollment we went to a school named, Fair Garden Elementary and everyone was very nice to us. There were kids all around the neighborhood so we met some good friends and the Freeman family would always introduce us as "our children"; not once did they refer to us as "foster children".

Every Sunday we would go to Sunday school and church at Tabernacle Baptist Church. It was a big church and a lot of the women wore hats which I thought was silly, but I didn't have to wear one. It was such a wonderful life living with this family. My eleventh birthday, they gave me a party with gifts and daddy came over. They knew my daddy well and he told us that he asked the courts to put us with this family, which I know now, had to be a GOD moment.

I went to the library for the first time and I got a library card. That started my desire to read like never before. They allowed us to

15

walk places by ourselves. We got bicycles and they even put a swing set in the backyard. It was like all of our dreams were coming true. There was a grape vine on the fence, an apple tree and a cherry tree in the backyard. They also had a garden, which I didn't like because we had to go and pick greens and tomatoes and shell beans, but they were good when we ate them!

We were introduced to more of the family members who lived close by, Aunt Almeda and Uncle Jack. Aunt Almeda was a beautician and she would wash, press and curl my hair often; I always looked forward to that. They made sure my brother's hair was always cut and neat; I must say that they had us looking sharp. They even bought us nice clothes, not hand-me-downs; but if they were, they sure didn't look like it. I can't tell you how truly happy we were. This family was amazing to us, everyone was. We were disciplined in a loving manner and they would always talk to us and explain what we did wrong and how we should correct it.

The punishments were always explained and they would show us scriptures in the Bible about being honest and the character we should live by to become trustworthy young adults. Ms. Freeman showed us the belt and switch she would use on our behind if we crossed the lines and were unruly.

I can remember only once when we both got our behinds tore up. We were playing in the living room, throwing something as we were fussing at each other about the channel on the TV. I wanted to watch Lost in Space but my brother wanted to watch Star Trek. So we hit each other and my brother punched me in the mouth knocking my two front teeth up in my gums. Blood went everywhere, they rushed in to see what was wrong; they beat his butt for that and told him he never should hit a girl!! They took me to the hospital and the doctors had to set my teeth back and it caused me to have a gap. When my daddy heard about it he came to the house and he put my brother on his lap and whipped his butt again, however; this time he spanked my legs with the switch and told me not to ever fight my brother. I did punch him in the eye but it wasn't hard enough to do any damage. We never fought each other again! We lived there until I was nineteen and my brother was eighteen. Now the real world began to form so get ready for this wild and crazy ride.

Chapter 5 Teen and High School Life

Growing up in this caring family didn't change the basic rules for a teen. These people were extra strict on us, they had rules that we refused to disobey simply due to the consequences they clearly explained. They didn't have to discipline us often because following the rules wasn't hard. We had our household chores and we had to wash and iron our own clothes. I ironed my brother's clothes because he was dangerous with the iron, he would always turn it up too high.

Even though all of the adults in the house were over the age of 35, we were treated like kids. They allowed us to make mistakes without reminding us of them. I will tell you some very defining moments as a teen and as a senior in high school. Attending Park Junior, I was a smart student, I enjoyed doing homework, and reading was my favorite hobby. I had some great friends and we hung out a lot on the weekends. We enjoyed going to the skating rink, movie theatre, the park, the zoo, and other places where we would have fun.

We did a lot of walking to school and riding our bikes to each other's house. Being a "foster teen" wasn't too bad of a life. My "family" made sure that I wore the nicest clothes and my hair was done every month. The birthday celebrations were a big deal with them and that really made me feel extra special.

Entering High school life was fun; I was in the marching band as the best flag girl ever! That was my escape from the world of being a normal teen. No one ever teased me about my situation and everyone I was close to knew about it. One thing though, throughout high school, I didn't have a boyfriend; probably because I was real skinny and wore glasses. Therefore, I put a lot of time into studying! Being a late bloomer I did something really silly one summer when I was about sixteen.

A lot of my friends had healthy busts, so I decided to put a pair of socks in my bra and it looked like I had grown over the summer. I will never forget how real it looked and all of my friends were amazed and the boys started to notice me. I know it was silly, but I wanted that attention from the boys. It worked for a few weeks. One day we had a long gym period and we played volleyball which made me sweat badly, so I had to shower and change after gym. I had forgotten to bring a clean pair of socks. Wow talk about an embarrassing day! I had to pull my sweater over me, but everyone noticed and they teased me about it for months. I went back to my normal, small, self.

Becoming a woman was handled so delicately with my family; they sat me down and explained everything to me. They kept harping on the fact that if a boy ever touches me I could become pregnant. They put so much fear in me I thought I would NEVER let that happen, right? OOPS... At the age of eighteen, for my birthday, I lost my virginity and the proof was in the sheets. They turned red and I was so scared. Hey, it was only ONE time so there was no way I would get pregnant. Besides, the boy I was with told me that it wouldn't happen because the sheets changing color meant that I wasn't going to become pregnant. I know it's stupid but I was a very naive young girl... of course I believed him!

About one month later it was time for my physical and when the doctor looked at me, he shook his head and was telling me that my hymen was broken; meaning that I had had sex. I was shocked! Then, he nicely explained to me that I was pregnant!! I cried out that it couldn't be possible because I just did it that once and I will never do it again. That was quite a defining moment in my life. I was snatched out of my protective teen life and thrown into the pregnant "bad girl" circle. The only thing I knew was to sit my family down and tell them what happened. So I called a meeting with them and they hugged me and cried and then the "serious talk" began. This family showered me with love and told me that I have two options. I could go to a girl's home for unwed mothers and they will teach me how to be a mother to help me to get my life back on track or I could put the baby up for adoption and continue with my life because I had a scholarship for Business College and wanted to go. I was waiting for another option but they told me that abortion was not in their vocabulary and they would not support that.

I was so hurt, here I was an eighteen year old pregnant high school senior, fearful of what to do. Well, when I told my father, he cried and cried but he told me how much he loved me and that he would be there for me. The big shock of all came when I called my mother with the news. She told me that I didn't need a baby and she would pay for an abortion. So that's what I did, yes, I committed an ugly, awful, shameful crime! On the day of the procedure I still didn't know where or how my mother came up with the $200.00, but she did.

That was a very scary day for me, I felt horrible and afraid. Ms. P., my social worker, had called me to tell me that she loved me and would come see me soon. I couldn't talk to her or anyone, I was quiet for about two days. The family fixed me soup and made sure I ate and was doing ok. At night when I went to bed, during my sleep, I would hear a baby crying and wake up to find no baby. I even thought about suicide, and what happens to a "foster youth" getting close to "aging out" of the state care title. All of my dreams were erased and I thought of how I had maintained good grades in high school and graduated with a 3.5 GPA. I had dreams of attending Business College and becoming an accountant and furthering my career.

Life did get a little better after a while. I attended the prom with a friend and he took me out to eat at Shoney's. We met up with some other friends, no one talked about what had happened to me; but I knew most of my classmates had heard about it. Graduation came and I was doing well. I enrolled in Draughon Business College and started

20

classes. Wow! It was going well and my family would help me with money sometimes. During this transition I found out about living on your own.

My father brought me a red Chevy Chevette and I moved into my own apartment. The state was helping me a little and my scholarship was a great blessing, but I also got a part-time job as a cashier/clerk at a convenience store. The first semester was great and I was excelling in all my classes.

Chapter 6 My First Real Detour

Being in Business College was truly a heartfelt desire that I really enjoyed. I was functioning quite well and had no more nightmares of a baby crying. My family would call me every week and invite me over for dinner on the weekends when I didn't have to work. Low and behold, I met a guy named A.W., he was tall, dark, and handsome! He was a little older than me and was an outstanding car mechanic. I met him at my convenience store and we started hanging out. I introduced him to my family and they liked him, but they thought he was too old for me; I was eighteen and a half and he was twenty-three.

He was my first real boyfriend and he was fine as wine. He started out as a gentleman and took me out to eat at nice restaurants. Of course this was new to me. Here I was a plain Jane country girl and this fine man was interested in me, whoa! I ended up being with him and that is when all the abuse started. He tried to control me and did not want me talking to other male classmates. I didn't see anything wrong with it because he was the only boyfriend I had.

One morning while preparing for class, one of my classmates had car troubles and wanted to know if he could catch a ride with me. He lived in an apartment building close to me so he walked to my apartment and waited outside by my car. Oh my goodness, A. W. came outside to walk me to my car and started cussing at the guy for standing beside my car! Then, he wanted to know why he had placed his books on top of my car. He tried to explain things to A.W. and so did I. Well A.W. slapped me in the face and my nose started bleeding. The guy ran to another apartment and banged on the door to call the police, no one had cell phones then. I couldn't believe it!

The police arrived and I went to a neighbor's apartment where this couple calmed me and treated me nicely. My classmate stayed there with me to tell what happened. The police talked to A. W. and he said he was just jealous and thought something different, which was a lie because we told him the truth. Well I was late for class that morning and I apologized to my classmate. Things went downhill fast after that first incident. A.W. became verbally abusive to me and started calling me names like "smart ass" and "little miss perfect ass". He would tell me that I thought I was better than him, which was not true!

The whole relationship started to take a lot from me and my grades slipped from A's to B's then C's. One weekend my friend L.M. was over with her boyfriend, we were playing cards and A.W. got upset about something; he grabbed me and threw me up against the wall which caused my small wall clock to fall on my head. This, in turn, caused my nose to bleed again! My friend L.M. called my daddy on the phone and her boyfriend took A.W. outside the apartment.

I wanted him out of my life because it was no longer a safe relationship. Well, my father came over and the police came also. That day my father pulled his gun on A. W. and told the policeman that he could take him to jail once he shoots A.W. I was too scared and didn't want my father to go to jail over me and my stupid choices. I stood in front of my dad and begged him not to shoot A.W. because we were through and I would never see him again. The policeman told A.W. to leave my apartment and never return or he would go to jail.

He left and my friend L.M. and her boyfriend stayed with me until I went to sleep. I couldn't get my mind back on my classes, it was too hard to focus on my work. The rest of the semester I made B's and Cs. This was not me, I never made C's so I wanted to do something else and move away from Knoxville. While I was watching television I saw the commercial saying "Army, be all you can be", I did want to travel so I decided to put in the paperwork to join the Army. I was nineteen and ready to move away!

This is when I learned the true spelling of my first name. I had to get my original birth certificate and I cried when I saw it because all my life I thought my name was Vanessa, but it was Venasta! Finding out that information made me feel so different about my life, who was I really? I was going to have a new start with a new name. Well, my family was so excited for me to join the Army; my dad was a little sad and my brother was really sad. My brother was getting caught up in the street life and felt he might not ever see me again.

I was way excited, my siblings and mother just said it was a good idea and to be safe. We never hugged each other goodbye, but my foster family gave me a little going away party. They hugged and kissed me and Ms. P. was there also. Everyone made sure I had an address book, stamps, ink pens and envelopes and a lot of writing paper, remember this was 1979, no cell phones.

Chapter 7 Army Life

The long ride to Fort Dix, New Jersey on that Greyhound bus was full of anticipation. I met so many people just like me, starting out on our first adventure away from home. After listening to me talk, I was nicknamed Tennessee because of my deep southern, country accent. There was no time for feeling alone because all of us were excited about basic training and we talked about our families.

When I told them that I was a foster child due to my mother being burned to death in a fire, it caused them to be very sympathetic towards me. I was treated extra nice and even though I knew it was wrong to lie like that, I didn't care because I didn't want anyone to know the truth. I felt like people would look at me differently; like this pitiful, troubled girl who nobody wanted to be friends with. I could hear those mean words in my head from Ms. M., "you'll never amount to anything and nobody wants you, not even your own mother".

Basic training was hard, I cried a lot and called my daddy every weekend. My drill sergeant was mean as a snake but he treated us all the same. I was so glad to complete basic training and then go to Fort Lee, Virginia for school as a supply clerk, 76-Delta. Believe it or not, the guy who I had dated when I was in Business College, A. W., was there!

I was so surprised to see him and of course the memories of being with him were clearly embedded in my mind. My heart ached a little because I felt like I still loved him! We became close once again. But weeks later he told me he had a girlfriend who had just finished her military school and she was pregnant with his child! I was devastated. Anyway, he apologized to me for using me and he said he was going to marry her. Later on, it was on the local news that a military man was arrested for beating his wife; she was in a coma and they had a little baby boy that was unharmed.

Oh my goodness, it was A.W., wow! He was sent to Ft. Leavenworth and that's all I ever heard about him. I was so thankful that it wasn't me; once again I was "snatched out" of an abusive relationship and "thrown into" the military life. You can imagine the lifestyle of freedom I experienced! I loved going to the bowling alley and to the club on weekends to dance and have non-alcoholic drinks with my buddies. My favorite was the Strawberry Daiquiri and Piña Colada, we all became close just like a family.

I was beginning to get used to my nickname, "Tennessee", and I was pretty popular! Graduation time from Material Supply Course came and I was receiving my sharpshooter's badge for the M16. It had me feeling pretty proud, even as a "foster child". I didn't have any family members at the ceremony, but I still felt good about what I had accomplished! Later, I put in for overseas duty but it didn't happen. I had 30 days of leave before going to Ft. Bragg, North Carolina. I kept in touch with my family and they had kept my car for me, so of course that's where I went. They treated me special as always. I went to see my mother and sister but it wasn't a welcomed visit. I was just so glad to have been snatched away from that environment, she acted like she was glad to see me but I didn't trust her.

I still received no kisses or hugs, but I didn't want to give them to her anyway. However, she did introduce me to some of her co-workers. The strangest thing was they had never heard of me and kept saying, "I didn't know you were her daughter"; all my mother would say was that I was her oldest child. I saw my brother Terry, he was living with my father but doing crazy things. He was hanging with the wrong crowd and running the streets late at night. I tried talking to him but he was in his rebellious state. He did say that he hated our mother for what she had done to us. I felt the same way a little, but sometimes I felt sorry for her.

I didn't have any connections with my other brother and sister. My mother showered my sister with love but she treated my brother, Khris, badly and never spoke positively about him. It was time to leave for Ft. Bragg! I drove by myself through the mountains, and I had no feelings of regret or sadness; I was just excited to start my new life. I vowed that I would never go back to see anyone but my father and the family who raised me.

Chapter 8 Being Me and Living Free

Fort Bragg was a huge base and I learned where the bad places were quickly. I lived in the female barracks and we had separate rooms. Most of the other soldiers were pretty friendly and four of my military school buddies were stationed there also. We became very close and stuck together like glue. I was still known as "Tennessee" but I was used to it so it wasn't a problem. Whenever I met new people and we discussed our family, I stuck to my story about my mother dying in a fire, leaving me in the foster care system.

Ms. Freeman passed away during my stay there at Ft. Bragg, the military allowed me to go to the funeral which was big; she was very well known in the east Knoxville community. I couldn't believe the freedom I felt being on my own, making my own decisions, and still being a productive young woman. I was very proud to be serving in our Armed Forces. Since I didn't have a "boyfriend", on the weekends, when anyone would go out I would stay in and iron their uniforms and they would pay me!

I always won best uniform during inspections and my boots were polished to the max. Every Friday I would get a three day pass for the best uniform in my platoon. Funny though, the pass started Friday after inspections and ended Sunday night, so I still had to be in formation on Monday mornings.

Some truly amazing things took place that could have put me in jail or hell while I was being me and living free, since I loved to go to the club on the weekend and dance! Some of my friends got together and went to a club on the post, it was called the Dragon Club back then. Well I was quite trusting of the people I hung with so while we were at the club I got up to dance and left my virgin drink glass on the table. I would always have one and I took a long time to drink it because they were expensive, I didn't drink beer until I got older.

I liked to be alert and in complete control wherever we went to party. I enjoyed dancing and after dancing I came back to the table and took ONE sip of my drink, it wasn't five minutes later; I felt dizzy and my vision was blurred. I screamed out to my friends that something was wrong, they stood me up to take me to the bathroom and I passed out!! They called the M.P. and I could hear them talking and asking me my name and my friends were ballistic. I felt dizzy and they walked me outside, the M.P. said that someone had slipped something in my drink; well I was mad as hell!!

I wouldn't think that someone would do that to me plus everyone at our table was a friend, or so I thought. That ended my clubbing days real fast!! I cried out to God and asked Him to save me from everything. I thought about my family back in Knoxville and how hurt they would be if I had died; especially my dad. Well time went by and low and behold one of our friends was celebrating her 21st birthday, all of us had turned 21. We went to the bowling alley and had beer and bowled all night long. I liked Michelob Lite and would usually have two. I took a long time to drink it because that was expensive for me and I didn't like spending my money that way.

Since the weekend was going to continue on from Friday night, that Saturday night our friend wanted to go to a club off post. We weren't too comfortable with that because the military had placed certain areas off limits for us. We decided to go to one anyway! It was somewhere off the busy side of town. This was such a shocking experience for me! We went to the bathroom area and I had noticed there was a long line.

I just thought it was for the bathroom but as we got further to the area there was a lady sitting at a desk with a notebook and a big bag with some little square plastic bags in it. Remember that I was naive about club life still and had no idea what was going on. She asked me what I needed and I told her just to use the bathroom and she said I was in the wrong line!! How about they were selling drugs, I freaked out! I started screaming and everybody looked at me laughing and calling me retarded!!

I ran out of the bathroom and back into the club area screaming, "They're selling drugs in there"! My friends grabbed me and we all went outside. I cussed them all out and told them I was leaving and so they called me a cab because they wanted to stay. But we all ended up leaving. No one had driven their cars due to the fact that we were going to be drinking beer; at least we had the sense not to drive. As we were leaving we saw police cars pulling up to the club. The ending of that story, there was a raid on that club! I could've ended up in jail for something I was totally innocent of! Well that scared me straight from going to any club off the base.

I began spending most of my time in the barracks ironing BDUs (battle dressed uniforms) on weekends making extra money. The day came when I met my future husband. I was in the mess hall's dinner line and this guy kept staring at me, I tried to be cute and kept pushing my glasses up on my face. He was tall, brown skinned and handsome! Once inside the dining hall we were separated but my friends made a big scene and yelled out there was a star in the place named "Tennessee" and pointed at me, everybody looked at me and started clapping and mocking my name.

I stood up and took a bow and that's when he came over and sat with me. So we became a hot couple and I was crazy about this guy. His name was Terry, which made me very comfortable with him because that was my brother's name. He was a great basketball player and had the nickname of "ice-man". He was in the 364th Petroleum Company and I was in the 249th Supply Company. I went to all of his company basketball games. Do I need to say more? He took me to meet his family in Waycross, GA. Talk about country! They were really sweet and we all got along well.

Low and behold I became pregnant and when I told him he was so happy and he wanted to marry me! The only thing was that I was coming up for promotion and the end of my 3 years; I wanted to stay in the Army but he didn't want me to stay. He told me he would stay in and take care of me and our baby! After enduring the relaxed pregnant life, my baby girl was born on September 7, 1982.Three weeks later, I was honorably discharged. I was so thankful to have a beautiful healthy baby, the labor was something, and I had natural birth...whew! We moved in together in a nice little apartment off post and were married two months later at the courthouse on November 5, 1982.

Chapter 9 Being a Military Wife

So I was Mrs. M. and I felt so good having a husband, baby and nice apartment. There were many times that I reflected on my childhood and I had prayed that I would be a loving mother and never ever allow my daughter to be around my mother alone. My mother did send me boxes of clothes for her first grandbaby. My husband and I lived pretty good until one day we received some mail stating that he had a baby girl who was born earlier that year, June to be exact! My, what an ugly storm to hit me. Of course he denied it, but the truth came out and he did indeed have another daughter.

I can't even tell you the devastation of that time frame. All I know is we went to court and I met the other woman and her baby. All I did was shake my head because I was stunned! I kept thinking how could he do something so low down and dirty to me? Oh I used the d-word, not deliverance, the h-word, not hallelujah and I called him an a-hole, not anointed. He was apologetic, but I just couldn't get it out of my mind; however, divorce never came out of his mouth or mine. I guess we both were still madly in love with each other and he treated me like a queen for many years afterwards.

Many months of frustration hit me in the face; the adultery and the lies became overwhelming, however; I stayed in a state of prayer! God worked miracles in our relationship; our marriage began to blossom. I started going to this Baptist church in Spring Lake, N.C. I met some wonderful women and couples there. I joined that church and started learning more about the Bible, I loved reading but I didn't do much praying.

One Easter Sunday the church was filled to capacity and even the top balcony area was full. I remember crying out to God, asking Him to help me. Then all of a sudden this mist was moving towards me. My stomach was feeling funny and I thought I was losing my mind! I looked around at those sitting close to me but no one seemed to notice.

This mist rested on my lap and I felt this enormous wave of wind hit my face and heat rose on me. I jumped up and screamed out loud and my lips felt numb, but fat! I was trying to talk but mumbling something and I ended up standing outside of my pew in the aisle with my hands lifted up! Wow such an embarrassing moment! When I opened my eyes the entire church was looking at me, the Pastor had come down from the pulpit and was standing in front of me with his arms folded looking at me!

Everyone just stared at me as if they were afraid of me! I wanted to grab my daughter and run out of there but I couldn't move. This lasted for about three minutes. No one said a word and I just stood there crying and shaking. The Pastor lifted his hands and looked at me smiling and said that he hadn't seen that in years! I had no idea what he meant, however, an older lady came to me and put her arms around me and told me that no one can take what God had given me. I wanted to know what "it" was and what had really happened to me. The lady walked me back to my seat and some people on that pew got up and moved away from me, no joke!

When church was over I left out with my daughter and no one said anything to me! I got home and told my husband that I lost my mind and he needed to take me to a psychiatrist because I started hearing this voice saying things like, "you're okay, I am here" but I just didn't know! That night I looked in the mirror and saw fingerprints over my heart. I screamed and went to show my husband. He didn't know what was happening. I wanted to go to the doctor but I was too afraid that they might admit me to the psycho ward.

I called the Pastor and told him he better explain what happened to me or I was leaving that church. All he said was that it was a GOD touch and he couldn't elaborate on it. He assured me that it was the Holy Spirit, but I did not know who or what that was. As I continued reading the Bible, I started to pray more and my relationship with Jesus intensified. I knew and understood the baptism of the Holy Spirit and began walking in some serious power! At church people would just look at me when I came in.

All I knew is that my prayers were being answered quickly. My husband was at peace and my daughter was just as obedient as ever! It was during this time I met a sister named Beverly P., she had asked me to be her prayer partner. I politely told her that I don't pray a whole lot and that she would be doing most of the praying. But she insisted that the Lord had told her it was to be me! We have been friends now for over 30 years and pray together often!

Life was happy with our family and then, my husband received orders for Korea, UGH! He had to leave me in the U.S. just as I found out I was pregnant! He was too thrilled and said he was praying for a son! Well my daughter told me that she was praying for a brother, low and behold, we had a son on December 25, 1988!

My husband was still in Korea when our son was born. While there, he had affair with another woman. I did not understand what was happening to us! Oh, I found out about it because she called my house! I waxed stronger in my prayer life and began praying for other marriages, strange things began to happen. Husbands got saved, filled with the Holy Spirit, and delivered from their sinful ways, but nothing like that was happening in my marriage! My husband returned to a comfortable environment, of course he apologized, cried and pleaded for forgiveness. Since I was such a love blinded-wife; standing on my faith for our marriage, I forgave him and remained married to him.

My husband received orders for GA, we were stationed at Hunter Army Airfield in Savannah and it was nice! I met Pastor G. Keller and his family, and began attending and joined their church.

They were a very worshipful congregation and I developed beautiful relationships with many of the people there. He told me once during a prayer service that I had this gift called intercession. There were times of great prayer and people were getting their prayers answered quickly, all I knew was I would pray the Word of God and He would perform mightily.

Life was getting better and in 1990 we had our third child, a precious daughter, Shanae. She was so beautiful and quite healthy. I was so amazed at how the Lord had allowed me to have such healthy children, being that I had done such a horrendous thing at the age of eighteen. You can imagine how good I felt being the mother of three beautiful healthy children! As time went on, the joy of motherhood was extremely precious to me and I did everything with my children.

Well, once I was visiting a church and they had a "prophet" there who was fired up and speaking words to quite a few people. Shanae was sitting on my lap, my other two were sitting next to me. He looked at me and said this, "lady I know that you are tired of babies, but the Lord is going to give you ONE MORE" wow I was ticked, he looked me right in my face and said again, "the Lord said that you are going to have one more."

I wanted to slap him in the face and I said that he was a false prophet! I had no intention of having another baby, I was done. I can laugh out loud now because in February of 1992 I gave birth to my last child. The Lord had told me I was going to have a boy and to name him Emmanuel, which I did. Here I was, a healthy mother with four beautiful, healthy children; two born in NC and two born in GA. Funny that both Shanae and Emmanuel had the same doctor and both were born by cesarean at the same hospital, Memorial Health, only God could have done this.

Chapter 10 More Painful Infidelity

We started to bring healing to our marriage, or so I thought, but my husband continued to be unfaithful. A short time after our last son was born he received orders for Germany! While I was still recuperating at the hospital, he had a woman in our home. My friends told me about it and I was just too through! I decided to focus on my children and just be active in church, ignoring him as much as possible. Unfortunately, we lived in the same house without any type of emotional or physical ties, I hated him and I refused to allow him to touch me.

On the other hand, I was very excited to go to Germany and he wanted us to accompany him. He left about two months before us, so I had the grand experience of flying overseas with four small children on the Fourth of July! Germany was an exciting experience, I did so much with our children because my husband was usually in the field for weeks. We were in Dexheim, close to the Nierstein River. Once I became so depressed with the marriage I did something so crazy I can't believe I actually had the mindset for it.

As shocking as it may be, I actually planned to commit suicide by driving into the Nierstein River! I had put my younger kids in the back seat and my oldest was in the front seat. They were all sleeping. I pulled up on the shore and backed my car up facing the river. All I could think of was that we were going to be in heaven and I would not have to see my husband ever again. The scariest experience happened, there was a large being walking across the sand right before the river; he was tall and very bright, maybe wearing a long shirt or something.

Anyway, he looked right at me and his eyes seemed to move up close to my window, no lie! I was shaking so badly and he looked right in my mind and heart, I felt like he knew what I was planning to do. I just shook my head, started crying and asked out loud, "What is he doing out here this time of morning," it was about 2 or 2:30 A.M. I heard this voice say, "Why are YOU out here this time of morning?" I looked at my children all sleeping so peacefully and I had to start the car and leave. The being/man just stood there looking at me, as if he was waiting on me to leave. I didn't know if he was an angel, human or Jesus himself but that was an experience I will never forget.

However, since it wasn't meant for me to do something terribly stupid, I went on a three day fast and I asked the Lord to kill my husband in an accident. I was specific too, I asked God to make him have an accident in his fuel tanker. I asked that no one would be hurt, not his driver or anyone else. Believe it or not he had to do a fuel run to Bad Kreuznach, which had steep narrow roads and the drive was over 30 miles. I was shocked when his unit called me to tell me everything!

Something went wrong with their steering wheel and they ran off the road and turned over. His driver got out but he was pinned in and had to use his pocket knife to cut the thick seatbelt. I was so shocked I ran out on the balcony, looked up to heaven and yelled at God, "Since when do you listen to me?" I had promised the Lord that I would just move back to the States, remain celibate, raise my children and not grieve for him. But God had other plans of course.

I repented, cried out for forgiveness and the Holy Spirit spoke out loud and clear to me, "My daughter be careful of your words, they carry power". I was messed up after that for a few months, every time I was in church I would bow on my knees and worship, this is something I still do. We moved to Wiesbaden, where I met Pastor E. Freeman and his wife L., they were a powerful couple from Africa and he taught a lot on the Holy Spirit and worship.

We attended church there and I didn't like it in the beginning because they prayed all the time and had midnight prayers. I asked him why they did that because I would fall asleep every time. He told me that they were covering me in prayer and that the Lord was going to use me mightily, ok right? Ha! One time I told him I didn't want him to pray for me anymore, I was tired of it, but they ignored me and I kept coming back. Something was drawing me and I couldn't resist it. My husband started attending and for the first time, I saw this man on his knees crying out to God. Wow, talk about a Kodak moment! His relationship with God enriched our lives greatly.

Eventually, they ordained me as an evangelist. They gave me a certificate that stood out in my mind for a long time. I knew it meant my faith was going to be tried by fire and since fire burns paper, I couldn't allow it to define me! Yet everywhere I went, I would always talk to people about Jesus and pray for them on the spot right where we were. I had no fear or shame! One time I heard a voice in the kitchen that spoke to me saying, "I am not stupid, I am not dumb, I am God," somehow I fell against the fridge and slid down on the floor, losing water! I was so scared but at the same time, this big presence I felt was so calm and peaceful. However, I couldn't talk for a while.

In the meantime my marriage relationship was growing better and we started doing more things together as a family. Low and behold an ugly vicious attack hit me, I went to the doctor for a check-up and was told that I had something called chlamydia. They explained everything to me, I went off! I told them I have been a faithful wife always and didn't understand how I got that. Well, it was from my husband! They put me on antibiotics and I was livid! I told my husband he was a no good, dirty dog, but I used foul language again. I also told him that I wanted him out of my life as soon as we get back to the States! I prayed and anointed my body and God did heal me totally from it, but I was still angry!

Chapter 11 Georgia Life

We received orders back to the States and were stationed at Fort Stewart, GA. I instantly loved the area and we were blessed with our very first home, it was four bedrooms, just built and very nice! The Lord had His hands upon us. We had a wonderful neighborhood with fantastic neighbors. I found an awesome church to attend and met some very wise and powerful pastors once again, Phil and Judy B., it was so amazing. I became a Sunday School teacher for four and five year olds and continued teaching for ten years. Later, I was on the prayer/healing ministry team and had found my place of safety, refuge and peace.

As the years moved on, I became more determined than ever to be the mother that I never had. My focus was on pleasing the Lord, my children and very seldom my husband. Life was a lot better, my children were all in school and I wanted to be at home with them. So, I put in paperwork to have a home daycare for the state of Georgia for infants to five year olds. The process went smoothly and I did that for two years.

There was more to being a daycare provider than changing diapers. I spent time teaching the children the alphabet and counting numbers correctly. Their parents knew that I would pray over them and read scriptures. I was totally content working at home and being a full time mother. Throughout that time, my marriage was strictly on paper only. My husband continued to excel in his military career and I stayed the faithful wife, caring mother and genuine Christian woman. I must admit that I had the best times when my children and I would participate in church activities.

Sad to say, we didn't spend a lot of time with my husband, even though our Friday game nights were the best family bonding we had. He did teach the boys how to fish and use weapons correctly; his relationship with his children was always above and beyond. I am thankful that he was a good father to them and an awesome provider, but he was just a cheater!

After those two years working as a home daycare provider, I decided to work outside of the home. All of my children were in school doing well, and I was ready to pursue employment outside of being a home daycare provider. I started as a substitute teacher/educational aide for a DODDS elementary school. It's amazing how I worked mostly with kids having special needs, my heart was glad, I felt pretty solid in my job and things with my husband were somewhat normal.

I worked there 16 years and enjoyed it extensively. Since my husband was preparing for his 20 year military retirement, he was very supportive of whatever I wanted; he made sure the kids and I were comfortable with his career goals. He wanted to work in the juvenile/corrections field and so I prayed and prayed for him to be blessed with the position. God answered and he received that really good job, making good pay with excellent benefits.

Chapter 12 Final Betrayal

We were certainly not the most "together" couple, but I was able to maintain being a faithful, supportive, dedicated, "military wife" and an awesome mother. All thanks to the Holy Spirit and Word of God! As the children were dealing with middle school, high school and teen life, I stayed focused on church life and my job. My husband's retirement from the Army and quick transition to civilian life was smooth. He seemed to be more relaxed and treated me like he did when we first were married! I was in an ecstatic world of pure joy and all was going great!

BUT THEN…all of a sudden an arrow came. He was working twelve hour shifts which sometimes ran over. I believed it when he would tell me that he had double shifts sometimes. When I say, I had NO clue of anything crazy going on, and there was never a sign of unfaithfulness. Exposure came one morning when his job called to confirm a change of his shift. I told them that he had left earlier for work but they said that he wasn't there because he wasn't scheduled to work then.

Of course I assured them that he went to work and was there. They put me on hold and checked with operations which informed me that, "Officer M. is not here". I was stunned because he left earlier that morning with his backpack, dressed in uniform and had his badge on. All day long my mind was full of confusion. When I finally realized that he could be lying to me I became so upset. I called his job later that day when he was there. I calmly told him what happened and that I knew he wasn't at work. I also told him that he is no longer welcome in our home and to give me the house keys when he gets off. He didn't deny anything, just said, "Okay" and hung up the phone.

I waited for him on the front porch later that night. I will not lie, I wanted to punch him in the face and even kick him a few times; but I just sat there and cried and prayed. He pulled up and as soon as he got out of his car, he said he was sorry and he was glad that the truth came out because he was tired of living a double life! He gave me the house keys, apologized again and all I could say was, "go and be with whoever she is, I will be fine, and I am going to tell everyone in the family about it." He walked away and pulled out of the driveway and pulled out of my life.

It was on Mother's Day when he came to get his clothes and other things he wanted. He finally told me that he wanted a divorce and was moving out. He had a meeting with me and three of our teens at the table. Our oldest daughter had already left home and joined the Navy. My husband told us that it was all his doings and that he loved me as their mother but wasn't happy in our marriage. He had been living with another woman in Savannah for quite a while. We didn't argue in front of our teens, but later on that day before he left, we had some serious words.

During this time, in our city of Hinesville; there were many shootings, domestic disputes and violence taking place, so the spirit of murder was running wild. One morning I had an ugly demonic encounter take place. My soon to be divorced husband had come by to get his last items and I was dressed for work waiting on his butt. Everyone had left for school. This amazing spiritual battle unfolded. He sat down in a chair and I was standing up over him, he looked me in the face and told me that he didn't want to be married to me anymore and that he was going to get a lawyer.

Now read this slowly because this is what took place as soon as he finished talking. Somehow time was frozen and neither one of us were moving or talking. I saw this shadow come from behind me shaped just like a human. It was black and had two yellow eyes. As I

43

stood there frozen in time and he was too, this shadow floated down the hallway and into the kitchen. I could actually see it form the shape of a hand and pick up one of the blue steak knives we had in the wooden block!

Then it floated back down to the room and it stabbed the knife into the back of my husband's right ear. Blood came gushing out and that's when I screamed out and everything came back to normal. I heard a voice say, "daughter, you can do this your way, or you can do this my way." I started crying and shaking so bad and all he could do was look at me and say, "something is wrong here, one of us is supposed to be laying in a pool of blood," I responded, "yes fool you!" We both just looked in each other's eyes and I lifted my hands up in total surrender and said, "Lord I will do this your way." So I told him that I will not fight but to go ahead and get a lawyer and we will go from there. WOW, what a spontaneous supernatural situation. He hugged me goodbye and left.

I had to substitute that day for Mr. B. Rose's fourth grade class and I cried all the way to work. When I got to the class, I wrote my name on the board, Ms. Myrick and most of the kids couldn't pronounce my name correctly. Well, this one particular student raised her hand and asked me, "is it okay to call you Ms. Miracle?" Oh my goodness I almost fainted! How in the world did she come up with that after what I had just gone through at my home? Tell me if that wasn't GOD indeed? Other students started calling me Ms. Miracle and it lasted until school was out for the summer. Wow, what a glorious way of God's love carrying me.

To think that I could have ended up in jail and my kids taken from me. I just have to thank the Lord for giving me a clear choice and showing me the enemy's plan. Time moved on, the divorce was finalized a little over a year later and I stayed in the home. He made sure I received the money I was awarded. Twenty-two years of my life was demolished on a few sheets of paper and black ink. We signed and it was as if it never happened. The pain hit me so strong that I was hospitalized for twenty-four hours with a major UTI brought on by stress. I was shocked again that something could cause my body to respond like that.

My mental and emotional state was shaky, I found myself calling out to Jesus daily and I didn't want to talk to anyone. I knew that I had to be strong for my teens and it was GOD alone who carried me through. I remained single and celibate for five years after the divorce, remember that five is the number of grace. I wasn't used to the "single" life. So I guess grace was running out for my standing strong in being celibate because during that sixth year something really heart-tugging happened to me.

Chapter 13 Temptation Alley

The year that my oldest son graduated high school, 2007, became a serious type of crossing the borders for my own life. Here I was, minding my own business and celebrating my son's graduation party. A man approached me and asked if I was married, I smiled and said, "Oh no most definitely divorced". It just so happened that encounter led to dating a very nice gentleman who seemed to be well rounded in life. I explained to him that I had four seeds; two girls and two boys.

I also let him know up front that, "I am neither a booty call nor a piece of tail." I had to make it plain from the beginning! He said that he knew that and was interested in getting to know me, wow, what a strange feeling. We started going out to the movies and nice restaurants. I felt like a teenager all over again! I didn't think anyone would be interested in me since I was divorced with four seeds. The first month was wonderful! During the second month the big discussion came up about, "jumping the fence", that is what I called the subject of sex!

I explained to Mr. J. T. that I am celibate and believe that in a marriage there are neither yield signs nor stop signs with that famous word, "sex". However, in dating I put up a stop sign when it comes to that special arena. He thought I was playing at first but he got the message, or so I thought. Our times together were always good, safe ones. I began to feel pretty comfortable around him so I went to his house for dinner and a movie. Whoa what a test! I had to leave there and pray all the way home, yep it was just that serious.

No, I didn't give it up then either. Remember, five years of celibacy kept me in a safety zone, but having someone holding me and kissing me was way too much for me to contain. I had to think of how I wanted to continue with the relationship. I was falling for this man and so low and behold, one night I jumped the fence. Oh yes, I did and I felt so dirty afterwards. I burst into tears and he thought something was physically wrong with me and that maybe he hurt me. I told him that this is not something I do and I knew God was displeased with me.

The devil really hit me hard with that, I actually heard a loud voice tell me, "You're nothing but a slut and a whore". So I just cried out and said, "yes I am all of those things, but my God still loves me and He will get me through it." All I know, is instantly I felt this weight lift from me. We slowed up seeing each other so much after that and I was led by the Holy Spirit to go to the prayer room at my church and just lay it out in the presence of God.

After that, the Lord specifically spoke to my heart and told me to tell my pastors what I had done; no way was that God, right? I obeyed because I didn't want to be the one bringing sin in the camp like Achen in the Bible. Plus being on the prayer team, I didn't, couldn't, wouldn't lay hands on anyone because I refused to be the reason their prayers weren't heard and answered. Oh, I was sure my pastors would look down on me and I even told them that I was willing to go through any discipline they set in front of me. BUT GOD ALONE covered me with so much grace, all they did was let me know that God had forgiven me.

Need I say that I knocked that fence down again! I was all about pleasing my flesh. I enjoyed the attention and care he showed me. He introduced me to his family and people knew us as a couple. I realized I couldn't conquer it on my own. Honestly, a part of me didn't want to, but every time I thought about how Jesus died for me and I accepted Him; I felt guilty! But who do I talk to?

Most married couples were taking each other for granted twice a week, complaining about each other's shortcomings and quick to tell you to rebuke the spirit of lust. Wow, some of them walked heavily in that more than we single women. Then the single sisters carried so much anger and bitterness against men and I didn't want to be like that! Walking through that was an uncomfortable and difficult experience. I asked God to forgive me over and over again. I went through that each morning I woke up for about a month. I just didn't believe that I was totally forgiven.

What a lie from the devil himself! I know personally that we can run into the arms of the Lord when we mess up and purposely roll around in the mud, and He picks us up and showers us with His love! He did it for me and He will do it for you too. The next step was to inform my four seeds about my derailment. I wanted them to know the truth and disarm the enemy of any power over me. It was a nervous time, but I spoke to my oldest while she was out to sea and she just told me that she loved me! When I told my oldest son, he said he was suspicious because I listened to the Isley Brothers a lot! I told my youngest daughter and she just hugged me and asked if I was I okay. I didn't have to tell my youngest son because his older brother explained it!

Wow, this is why I call my crew "the fantastic four"! I apologized to them for not being that Godly mother example as I should. I wanted them to know that I too, could make selfish choices. So Mr. J.T. decided to break up with me because I refused to meet his fleshly needs. I was devastated because I thought he would want a woman who believed as I did. Three months went by and we didn't talk to or see each other.

I was greatly blessed by a couples' testimony about a 12 step program called, C.R. which meant Celebrate Recovery, but my Shanae said it just means Christian rehab. Oh well, I was a Christian and I needed rehabilitation! It was an awesome six to eight week program. I became more confident in my salvation and relationship with Christ by opening up and dealing with the truth about my "jumping the fence". I would encourage anyone to Google it and look at the testimonies from so many who have been through it. This was the most freeing experience I have walked through and I am so thankful for it.

One nice day and three months of no communication, Mr. J.T. called me and said he needed to talk with me, so I met him in a public place. He let me know that being celibate was new to him but he was willing to try since he had developed strong feelings for me. I must admit I had fallen for him as well, so I took on the challenge. We were doing really well and he respected my wishes. He ended up asking me to marry him! All I could think of was, "it's better to marry than to burn," so I said yes.

Chapter 14 Temporary Fairytale

Saying "I Do" the second time was a pretty good deal, September of 2009 was the most intoxicating time for me. I floated on clouds simply because I was getting married! Nothing else really mattered. We didn't have the same mindset for being a Christian, he believed in God but I was much more into the Word than he was. He was a religious man where I was more relational. Our beliefs held us at an awkward stance.

Yes we got married and had a lovely wedding, I kept thinking, "it's better to marry than to burn". My Pastor gave us pre-marital counseling, we really didn't have any major issues at that time. Mainly because I understood him to be a grown man; I was neither his boss nor his mother, and of course, he wasn't my father. I knew that I could not be GOD to him, yet I wish he was more into the Word than I was. Pastors T. and C. made sure I understood my role as his wife and when they married us, I took the vows to heart and I believed he did also.

During the first year we were heavily into spending time together. Our living together was somewhat of a small challenge, I worked days and he worked nights. Truth be told, I loved my time alone and that's why I had my own bedroom and he had his. I know it sounds crazy but you see being an intercessor meant that sometimes, I was awakened to pray not play and he didn't understand that. I wasn't about to give up my precious time spent with Abba Father just to please him, maybe if he was more of a praying man it would've been different. But I did know that before I married him, so my bad judgment call did cost me.

I longed to have someone praying with me and for me, but I settled for a comfortable companionship without a pure relationship which caused a sunken ship. Seriously, the marriage was just okay not really as loving as it started out to be. I did see the flashing caution lights, but I didn't know where my mind was most of the time. Somewhere torn between the saying, "It's better to marry than to burn" and "living single".

We were in the process of buying a nice home, we had the rent to buy option which was good for us. However, I desired to be better in my employment avenue, therefore; I enrolled in an online school to attain my Associates degree in accounting. Remember, this was my high school dream! So I was a planner and had counted the cost of my decisions. As life moved on we were getting closer to the house being turned over from a rental to a buying deal.

Chapter 15 Rough Terrain

We were not getting along as well as we should, I was disappointed in his lack of communication and his self-centered attitude. I took into mind that this was a man, who had never been married and he had no children so the only person he had to be 100% concerned with all of his life, was himself. While trying to maintain a level head and warm heart in the marriage, things became hectic. He was caught up in working and fishing and I was caught up in my prayer life, church activities and online classes. We spent less and less time together doing fun things and neither one of us seemed to be interested in making plans to change it.

It was about four months before we were to sign the papers to buy the house when all hell broke loose! One morning I woke up to a bed with red sheets, I was surprised because it wasn't something I expected! I showered and told my husband to take me to the emergency room. They ran tests on me but couldn't find anything major. Test results showed another urinary tract infection attacked me and they told me to take two days off my feet, no work and they put me on antibiotics.

Wow this sounded so familiar! I called my job and informed them that I had a medical excuse for 2 days of rest. I prayed, anointed myself with oil and stayed in the bed. My husband was very caring and extra nice for those two days. When I called my job to get my schedule, I was told that someone in administration made a mistake with my name in the computer and I wasn't able to work or get my pay that was due to me until it was corrected. YES, this really happened and I remembered thinking about Job in the Bible when everything hit him.

My health was under attack, my job was in chaos, and this went on for a few months. Signing the house papers went down the drain because my income was held up; my husband became upset and blamed me for it all. He told me that he wanted a divorce. What in the world was happening this time? I had no fight left in me. I just threw my hands up and walked in my room and sat on my bed, this time I had no tears but felt a sense of relief.

Something amazing did happen though. One day my friend Charlene told me to go to the Liberty Chamber of Commerce building and get the magazine that lists the businesses in town that may be advertising accounting positions. This was a divine intervention of God because the day I went there I ran into Felecia, she was an accountant for a particular business and their office was there. She asked me if I was interested in a job and I yelled, "Yes"! Come to find out her office's accounting clerk was moving and she needed a replacement!

I cried and cried tears of joy! She trained me well and I really enjoyed working there. The school finally corrected my paperwork, but I could only work there two days a week because I worked the other job three days a week. I was happy to be making my own income once again. We had thirty days to be out of the house and I didn't know where we were going. I looked at apartments and he was looking for a place just for him. He literally abandoned me. My church members came to help me pack up my things, my furniture was placed in storage and I didn't have a clue of where I was going to be. I mentioned my housing situation to some close friends and they were looking at places for me too.

I had a wonderful friend, Eunice, who told me that I could move into her upstairs bedroom because her children were grown and gone. I was so touched, not only did I live there for three months, but she let me move my own bedroom furniture in to make me feel more comfortable. This dear friend never charged me one penny for anything. My body came under attack again and I found it difficult to walk. I thought it was arthritis attacking me once again. There were

53

times when I couldn't even get out of the bed without pain in my legs and sometimes they would lock up.

I was still working with DODDS but just moving slow. When I told my oldest daughter what was happening she said these words, "mom, maybe your brook has dried up there in Hinesville since all of us are grown now and no close family is there." Those words rang loud in my ears. I lived in Hinesville for sixteen years and felt like my life was being tossed around like a hot potato which no one wanted to be left holding.

Chapter 16 Health Scare

I moved to Florida in March of 2014, ready to work and start a new life. I moved in with my oldest daughter and life was extremely beautiful. I put in applications and had two interviews. I aced both interviews and was waiting for a phone call. Life felt good, I visited a great church and they had to get a wheelchair for me because my legs just wouldn't move even though I had driven myself there. This was way too weird for me. I went to the church two more Sundays and the same thing happened, I was a little upset about what was happening to me without any explanation.

June fourth, my daughter and I were going to the Navy Hair salon for my appointment. As we were walking across the sidewalk a pain shot up my left leg and it froze! I couldn't move and began to fall back, I screamed out which caused my daughter to drop her wallet and grab me. My head felt strange and I had no idea what was happening, but after my hair appointment my daughter took me to urgent care.

The doctor had me walk in a straight line which I couldn't do, so they said that I needed to go to the emergency room immediately. My walking was not straight and I was moving slowly. I was a little confused because I had no pain but my legs felt heavy. Once at the Baptist South Health Hospital they kept me and ran tests. Little did I know, I would be there for six days! They found from MRIs that MS Relapse and ataxia had attacked me and I had lesions on my brain and back. This was a total shock but I told my neurologist and other doctors that I heard them and saw the photos, yet I still believe God will heal me.

Yes, I did drop a tear from each eye, I couldn't understand what was happening to me. I Googled everything I could find about ataxia and MS Relapse. It was quite shocking to see how it attacks the central nervous system and the spinal cord. During my hospital stay I continued with my live online classes and I would sing every morning and at night. A lot of the nurses and assistants wanted to come in my room to sit for about fifteen minutes because they said that my room "felt so peaceful". Well I let them know that the presence of the Lord was with me.

I met some amazing people while I was there but I was so happy when I was cleared to leave. The doctors told me that I needed to put in for disability, which was a huge shock! I think the worst thing about it all was that I couldn't drive for eight weeks, which turned into five more months!! These months had me feeling totally isolated from the world. However, when I found out about the Clay County Disability Bus system, I was more relaxed. I looked forward to going to my doctor's appointments because I met some wonderful people on the bus.

I would encourage and pray with everyone I met, speaking life to their conditions and situations. The main thing I shared with whomever was riding that day was, "we are VIPs and have a great chauffeur service," this caused loads of laughter for the bus drivers also. When you see and hear of others situations it causes you to become extremely grateful for your life! I began to spend more time reading my Bible and praying all the healing scriptures I could find.

These times were so special and the presence of the Lord would just engulf me. I didn't entertain any negative thoughts concerning the "medical condition" and I just confessed, "I'm not denying what I see, but it's not controlling me." So now, in 2019, my life is great. I am presently taking one medication and lots of vitamins. I have a VIP parking tag that puts me up front wherever I go and I have a nice black cane to assist me with walking. I have graduated with my Bachelors' in Accounting and I'm just waiting to see what the next journey in my life will be.

During these last five years, the Lord has blessed me to have two of my fantastic four living here in the same city and it gives us some beautiful family time. This is my life story and I am thankful to be able to share it. I pray that something you have read has encouraged your heart, strengthened your mind, and even made you laugh. Thank you for reading "Snatched out! Thrown In!"

Special Thanks

Special thanks to the fifth floor staff at Baptist Medical Center South in Jacksonville, FL. They were a great blessing to me. Thanks so much to my neurologist, Dr. Ravi Ponde and his wonderful staff I will always remember how kind and patient you were to me. Greater blessings to YOU dear reader!! Venasta, AKA, Vee.

GOD'S AMAZING PLAN UNFOLDS!!

Wow! I can't close out the ending without sharing what Abba Father has given me in Spite of it all!! God has blessed me with a wonderful, anointed man of God as my husband! Yes, I was married August 2018 and I have a new name, Venasta Parsons and for your information, he is a genuine, loving and supportive husband. God did an awesome work joining us together.

I may have another story in the future! Greater blessings of favor be upon you! Thank you so much for purchasing and reading Snatched Out! Thrown In!

To God be the Glory!

About the Author

Venasta was born and raised in Knoxville, TN and endured life as a foster child. She was blessed to be the mother of the "fantastic four", two sons and two daughters. She was a proud, United States Army Veteran and a born again Christian; not religious but relational.

Venasta decided to write this book after becoming a Guardian Ad Litem, Court Appointed Special Advocate for the states of Georgia and Florida. She thought about how her experience would make kids who she was assigned to feel more at ease and comfortable as she built and laid a foundation of trust.

Venasta started journaling in 2014. She was inspired by knowing others will see, feel and understand that real life happens to all of us. We just learn how to continue with tears, laughter and prayer! She truly believes there are a few more books within her to tell life's story from a real perspective because we live in a real world.

Venasta is finally believing, receiving and living a daily, supernaturally satisfied, married, life with her husband Joseph in Jacksonville, FL.